Dorothy Parker

SUNSET GUN

Dorothy Parker (1893–1967) was born in New Jersey and grew up in New York. In 1916, she sold some poems to *Vogue* and was given a job at the magazine writing captions for fashion photographs and drawings. Parker went on to become a drama critic at *Vanity Fair* and one of the most prominent members of the celebrated Algonquin Round Table. A famously witty speaker, she showed the same satiric gift in her book reviews for *The New Yorker* and *Esquire* and in her popular poems and stories.

BOOKS BY DOROTHY PARKER
IN VINTAGE CLASSICS

Enough Rope

Sunset Gun

SUNSET GUN

SUNSET GUN

Poems

Dorothy Parker

Vintage Classics
VINTAGE BOOKS
A DIVISION OF PENGUIN RANDOM HOUSE LLC
NEW YORK

FIRST VINTAGE CLASSICS EDITION 2024

The verses in this book were first printed in *The Bookman*, *The New Republic*, *The Nation*, *The New Yorker*, *Life*, *McCall's* magazine, *The Yale Review*, *New York World*, and *New York Post*.

Cataloging-in-Publication Data is available at the Library of Congress.

Vintage Classics Trade Paperback ISBN: 978-0-593-68540-2
eBook ISBN: 978-0-593-68541-9

vintagebooks.com

Printed in the United States of America
1st Printing

Contents

SUNSET GUN

GODMOTHER

The day that I was christened—
    It's a hundred years, and more!—
A hag came and listened
    At the white church door,
A-hearing her that bore me
    And all my kith and kin
Considerately, for me,
    Renouncing sin.
While some gave me corals,
    And some gave me gold,
And porringers, with morals
    Agreeably scrolled,
The hag stood, buckled
    In a dim gray cloak;
Stood there and chuckled,
    Spat, and spoke:
"There's few enough in life'll
    Be needing my help,
But I've got a trifle
    For your fine young whelp.

I give her sadness,
 And the gift of pain,
The new-moon madness,
 And the love of rain."
And little good to lave me
 In their holy silver bowl
After what she gave me—
 Rest her soul!

PARTIAL COMFORT

Whose love is given over-well
Shall look on Helen's face in hell,
Whilst they whose love is thin and wise
May view John Knox in paradise.

THE RED DRESS

I always saw, I always said
    If I were grown and free,
I'd have a gown of reddest red
    As fine as you could see,

To wear out walking, sleek and slow,
    Upon a Summer day,
And there'd be one to see me so,
    And flip the world away.

And he would be a gallant one,
    With stars behind his eyes,
And hair like metal in the sun,
    And lips too warm for lies.

I always saw us, gay and good,
    High honored in the town.
Now I am grown to womanhood. . . .
    I have the silly gown.

VICTORIA

Dear dead Victoria
    Rotted cosily;
In excelsis gloria,
    And R. I. P.

And her shroud was buttoned neat,
    And her bones were clean and round,
And her soul was at her feet
    Like a bishop's marble hound.

Albert lay a-drying,
    Lavishly arrayed,
With his soul out flying
    Where his heart had stayed.

And there's some could tell you what land
    His spirit walks serene
(But I've heard them say in Scotland
    It's never been seen).

THE COUNSELLOR

I met a man, the other day—
    A kindly man, and serious—
Who viewed me in a thoughtful way,
    And spoke me so, and spoke me thus:

"Oh, dallying's a sad mistake;
    'Tis craven to survey the morrow!
Go give your heart, and if it break—
    A wise companion is Sorrow.

"Oh, live, my child, nor keep your soul
    To crowd your coffin when you're dead." . . .
I asked his work; he dealt in coal,
    And shipped it up the Tyne, he said.

PARABLE FOR A CERTAIN VIRGIN

Oh, ponder, friend, the porcupine;
  Refresh your recollection,
And sit a moment, to define
  His means of self-protection.

How truly fortified is he!
  Where is the beast his double
In forethought of emergency
  And readiness for trouble?

Recall his figure, and his shade—
  How deftly planned and clearly
For slithering through the dappled glade
  Unseen, or pretty nearly.

Yet should an alien eye discern
  His presence in the woodland,
How little has he left to learn
  Of self-defense! My good land!

For he can run, as swift as sound,
　　　To where his goose may hang high;
Or thrust his head against the ground
　　　And tunnel half to Shanghai;

Or he can climb the dizziest bough—
　　　Unhesitant, mechanic—
And, resting, dash from off his brow
　　　The bitter beads of panic;

Or should pursuers press him hot,
　　　One scarcely needs to mention
His quick and cruel barbs, that got
　　　Shakespearean attention;

Or driven to his final ditch,
　　　To his extremest thicket,
He'll fight with claws and molars (which
　　　Is not considered cricket).

How amply armored, he, to fend
　　　The fear of chase that haunts him!
How well prepared our little friend!—
　　　And who the devil wants him?

BRIC-À-BRAC

Little things that no one needs—
　　Little things to joke about—
Little landscapes, done in beads,
　　Little morals, woven out,
Little wreaths of gilded grass,
　　Little brigs of whittled oak
Bottled painfully in glass;
　　These are made by lonely folk.

Lonely folk have lines of days
　　Long and faltering and thin;
Therefore—little wax bouquets,
　　Prayers cut upon a pin,
Little maps of pinkish lands,
　　Little charts of curly seas,
Little plats of linen strands,
　　Little verses, such as these.

INTERIOR

Her mind lives in a quiet room,
　　A narrow room, and tall,
With pretty lamps to quench the gloom
　　And mottoes on the wall.

There all the things are waxen neat
　　And set in decorous lines;
And there are posies, round and sweet,
　　And little, straightened vines.

Her mind lives tidily, apart
　　From cold and noise and pain,
And bolts the door against her heart,
　　Out wailing in the rain.

REUBEN'S CHILDREN

Accursed from their birth they be
Who seek to find monogamy,
Pursuing it from bed to bed—
I think they would be better dead.

FOR R. C. B.

Life comes a-hurrying,
　　Or life lags slow;
But you've stopped worrying—
　　Let it go!
Some call it gloomy,
　　Some call it jake;
They're very little to me—
　　Let them eat cake!
Some find it fair,
　　Some think it hooey,
Many people care;
　　But we don't, do we?

THERE WAS ONE

There was one a-riding grand
    On a tall brown mare,
And a fine gold band
    He brought me there.

A little, gold band
    He held to me
That would shine on a hand
    For the world to see.

There was one a-walking swift
    To a little, new song,
And a rose was the gift
    He carried along.

First of all the posies,
    Dewy and red.
They that have roses
    Never need bread.

There was one with a swagger
    And a soft, slow tongue,
And a bright, cold dagger
    Where his left hand swung—

Carven and gilt,
    Old and bad—
And his stroking of the hilt
    Set a girl mad.

There was one a-riding grand
    As he rode from me.
And he raised his golden band
    And he threw it in the sea.

There was one a-walking slow
    To a sad, long sigh.
And his rose drooped low,
    And he flung it down to die.

There was one with a swagger
    And a little, sharp pride,
And a bright, cold dagger
    Ever at his side.

At his side it stayed
    When he ran to part.
What is this blade
    Struck through my heart?

ON CHEATING THE FIDDLER

"Then we will have to-night!" we said.
"To-morrow—may we not be dead?"
The morrow touched our eyes; and found
Us walking firm above the ground,
Our pulses quick, our blood alight.
To-morrow's gone—we'll have to-night!

INCURABLE

And if my heart be scarred and burned,
The safer, I, for all I learned;
The calmer, I, to see it true
That ways of love are never new—
The love that sets you daft and dazed
Is every love that ever blazed;
The happier, I, to fathom this:
A kiss is every other kiss.
The reckless vow, the lovely name,
When Helen walked, were spoke the same;
The weighted breast, the grinding woe,
When Phaon fled, were ever so.
Oh, it is sure as it is sad
That any lad is every lad,
And what's a girl, to dare implore
Her dear be hers forevermore?
Though he be tried and he be bold,
And swearing death should he be cold,
He'll run the path the others went. . . .
But you, my sweet, are different.

FABLE

Oh, there once was a lady, and so I've been told,
Whose lover grew weary, whose lover grew cold.
"My child," he remarked, "though our episode ends,
In the manner of men, I suggest we be friends."
And the truest of friends ever after they were—
Oh, they lied in their teeth when they told me of her!

THE SECOND OLDEST STORY

Go I must along my ways
    Though my heart be ragged,
Dripping bitter through the days,
    Festering, and jagged.
Smile I must at every twinge,
    Kiss, to time its throbbing;
He that tears a heart to fringe
    Hates the noise of sobbing.

. . . .

Weep, my love, till Heaven hears;
    Curse and moan and languish.
While I wash your wound with tears,
    Ease aloud your anguish.
Bellow of the pit in Hell
    Where you're made to linger.
There and there and well and well—
    Did he prick his finger!

A PIG'S-EYE VIEW OF LITERATURE

*The Lives and Times of John Keats, Percy Bysshe Shelley,
and George Gordon Noel, Lord Byron*

Byron and Shelley and Keats
Were a trio of lyrical treats.
The forehead of Shelley was cluttered with curls,
And Keats never was a descendant of earls,
And Byron walked out with a number of girls,
But it didn't impair the poetical feats
Of Byron and Shelley,
Of Byron and Shelley,
Of Byron and Shelley and Keats.

Oscar Wilde

If, with the literate, I am
Impelled to try an epigram,
I never seek to take the credit;
We all assume that Oscar said it.

Harriet Beecher Stowe

The pure and worthy Mrs. Stowe
Is one we all are proud to know
As mother, wife, and authoress,—
Thank God I am content with less!

D. G. Rossetti

Dante Gabriel Rossetti
Buried all of his *libretti,*
Thought the matter over,—then
Went and dug them up again.

Thomas Carlyle

Carlyle combined the lit'ry life
With throwing teacups at his wife,
Remarking, rather testily,
"Oh, stop your dodging, Mrs. C.!"

Charles Dickens

Who call him spurious and shoddy
Shall do it o'er my lifeless body.
I heartily invite such birds
To come outside and say those words!

Alexandre Dumas and His Son

Although I work, and seldom cease,
At Dumas *père* and Dumas *fils,*

Alas, I cannot make me care
For Dumas *fils* and Dumas *père.*

Alfred Lord Tennyson

Should Heaven send me any son,
I hope he's not like Tennyson.
I'd rather have him play a fiddle
Than rise and bow and speak an idyll.

George Gissing

When I admit neglect of Gissing,
They say I don't know what I'm missing.
Until their arguments are subtler,
I think I'll stick to Samuel Butler.

Walter Savage Landor

Upon the work of Walter Landor
I am unfit to write with candor.
If you can read it, well and good;
But as for me, I never could.

George Sand

What time the gifted lady took
Away from paper, pen, and book,
She spent in amorous dalliance
(They do those things so well in France).

MORTAL ENEMY

Let another cross his way—
    She's the one will do the weeping!
Little need I fear he'll stray
    Since I have his heart in keeping.

Let another hail him dear—
    Little chance that he'll forget me!
Only need I curse and fear
    Her he loved before he met me.

PENELOPE

In the pathway of the sun,
In the footsteps of the breeze,
Where the world and sky are one,
    He shall ride the silver seas,
        He shall cut the glittering wave.
I shall sit at home, and rock;
Rise, to heed a neighbor's knock;
Brew my tea, and snip my thread;
Bleach the linen for my bed.
        They will call him brave.

BOHEMIA

Authors and actors and artists and such
Never know nothing, and never know much.
Sculptors and singers and those of their kidney
Tell their affairs from Seattle to Sydney.
Playwrights and poets and such horses' necks
Start off from anywhere, end up at sex.
Diarists, critics, and similar roe
Never say nothing, and never say no.
People Who Do Things exceed my endurance;
God, for a man that solicits insurance!

THE SEARCHED SOUL

When I consider, pro and con,
What things my love is built upon—
A curly mouth; a sinewed wrist;
A questioning brow; a pretty twist
Of words as old and tried as sin;
A pointed ear; a cloven chin;
Long, tapered limbs; and slanted eyes
Not cold nor kind nor darkly wise—
When so I ponder, here apart,
What shallow boons suffice my heart,
What dust-bound trivia capture me,
I marvel at my normalcy.

THE TRUSTING HEART

Oh, I'd been better dying,
    Oh, I was slow and sad;
A fool I was, a-crying
    About a cruel lad!

But there was one that found me,
    That wept to see me weep,
And had his arm around me,
    And gave me words to keep.

And I'd be better dying,
    And I am slow and sad;
A fool I am, a-crying
    About a tender lad!

THOUGHT FOR A SUNSHINY MORNING

It costs me never a stab nor squirm
To tread by chance upon a worm.
"Aha, my little dear," I say,
"Your clan will pay me back one day."

THE GENTLEST LADY

They say He was a serious child,
    And quiet in his ways;
They say the gentlest lady smiled
    To hear the neighbors' praise.

The coffers of her heart would close
    Upon their smallest word.
Yet did they say, "How tall He grows!"
    They thought she had not heard.

They say upon His birthday eve
    She'd rock Him to His rest
As if she could not have Him leave
    The shelter of her breast.

The poor must go in bitter thrift,
    The poor must give in pain,
But ever did she set a gift
    To greet His day again.

They say she'd kiss the boy awake,
        And hail Him gay and clear,
But oh, her heart was like to break
        To count another year.

THE MAID-SERVANT AT THE INN

"It's queer," she said, "I see the light
 As plain as I beheld it then,
All silver-like and calm and bright—
 We've not had stars like that again!

"And she was such a gentle thing
 To birth a baby in the cold.
The barn was dark and frightening—
 This new one's better than the old.

"I mind my eyes were full of tears,
 For I was young, and quick distressed,
But she was less than me in years
 That held a son against her breast.

"I never saw a sweeter child—
 The little one, the darling one!—
I mind I told her, when he smiled
 You'd know he was his mother's son.

"It's queer that I should see them so—
       The time they came to Bethlehem
Was more than thirty years ago;
       I've prayed that all is well with them."

FULFILMENT

For this my mother wrapped me warm,
And called me home against the storm,
And coaxed my infant nights to quiet,
And gave me roughage in my diet,
And tucked me in my bed at eight,
And clipped my hair, and marked my weight,
And watched me as I sat and stood:
That I might grow to womanhood
To hear a whistle and drop my wits
And break my heart to clattering bits.

DAYLIGHT SAVING

My answers are inadequate
To those demanding day and date,
And ever set a tiny shock
Through strangers asking what's o'clock;
Whose days are spent in whittling rhyme—
What's time to her, or she to Time?

SURPRISE

My heart went fluttering with fear
Lest you should go, and leave me here
To beat my breast and rock my head
And stretch me sleepless on my bed.
Ah, clear they see and true they say
That one shall weep, and one shall stray
For such is Love's unvarying law. . . .
I never thought, I never saw
That I should be the first to go;
How pleasant that it happened so!

SWAN SONG

First you are hot,
  Then you are cold;
And the best you have got
  Is the fact you are old.
Labor and hoard,
  Worry and wed,
And the biggest reward
  Is to die in bed.
A long time to sweat,
  A little while to shiver;
It's all you'll get—
  Where's the nearest river?

ON BEING A WOMAN

Why is it, when I am in Rome
I'd give an eye to be at home,
But when on native earth I be,
My soul is sick for Italy?

And why with you, my love, my lord,
Am I spectacularly bored,
Yet do you up and leave me—then
I scream to have you back again?

AFTERNOON

When I am old, and comforted,
    And done with this desire,
With Memory to share my bed
    And Peace to share my fire,

I'll comb my hair in scalloped bands
    Beneath my laundered cap,
And watch my cool and fragile hands
    Lie light upon my lap.

And I will have a spriggéd gown
    With lace to kiss my throat;
I'll draw my curtain to the town,
    And hum a purring note.

And I'll forget the way of tears,
    And rock, and stir my tea.
But oh, I wish those blessed years
    Were further than they be!

A DREAM LIES DEAD

A dream lies dead here. May you softly go
Before this place, and turn away your eyes,
Nor seek to know the look of that which dies
Importuning Life for life. Walk not in woe,
But, for a little, let your step be slow.
And, of your mercy, be not sweetly wise
With words of hope and Spring and tenderer skies.
A dream lies dead; and this all mourners know:

Whenever one drifted petal leaves the tree—
Though white of bloom as it had been before
And proudly waitful of fecundity—
One little loveliness can be no more;
And so must Beauty bow her imperfect head
Because a dream has joined the wistful dead!

THE HOMEBODY

There still are kindly things for me to know,
Who am afraid to dream, afraid to feel—
This little chair of scrubbed and sturdy deal,
This easy book, this fire, sedate and slow.
And I shall stay with them, nor cry the woe
Of wounds across my breast that do not heal;
Nor wish that Beauty drew a duller steel,
Since I am sworn to meet her as a foe.

It may be, when the devil's own time is done,
That I shall hear the dropping of the rain
At midnight, and lie quiet in my bed;
Or stretch and straighten to the yellow sun;
Or face the turning tree, and have no pain;
So shall I learn at last my heart is dead.

SECOND LOVE

"So surely is she mine," you say, and turn
Your quick and steady mind to harder things—
To bills and bonds and talk of what men earn—
And whistle up the stair, of evenings.
And do you see a dream behind my eyes,
Or ask a simple question twice of me—
"Thus women are," you say; for men are wise
And tolerant, in their security.

How shall I count the midnights I have known
When calm you turn to me, nor feel me start,
To find my easy lips upon your own
And know my breast beneath your rhythmic heart.
Your god defer the day I tell you this:
My lad, my lad, it is not you I kiss!

FAIR WEATHER

This level reach of blue is not my sea;
Here are sweet waters, pretty in the sun,
Whose quiet ripples meet obediently
A marked and measured line, one after one.
This is no sea of mine, that humbly laves
Untroubled sands, spread glittering and warm.
I have a need of wilder, crueler waves;
They sicken of the calm, who knew the storm.

So let a love beat over me again,
Loosing its million desperate breakers wide;
Sudden and terrible to rise and wane;
Roaring the heavens apart; a reckless tide
That casts upon the heart, as it recedes,
Splinters and spars and dripping, salty weeds.

THE WHISTLING GIRL

Back of my back, they talk of me,
  Gabble and honk and hiss;
Let them batten, and let them be—
  Me, I can sing them this:

"Better to shiver beneath the stars,
  Head on a faithless breast,
Than peer at the night through rusted bars,
  And share an irksome rest.

"Better to see the dawn come up,
  Along of a trifling one,
Than set a steady man's cloth and cup
  And pray the day be done.

"Better be left by twenty dears
  Than lie in a loveless bed;
Better a loaf that's wet with tears
  Than cold, unsalted bread."

Back of my back, they wag their chins,
    Whinny and bleat and sigh;
But better a heart a-bloom with sins
    Than hearts gone yellow and dry!

STORY

"And if he's gone away," said she,
"Good riddance, if you're asking me.
I'm not a one to lie awake
And weep for anybody's sake.
There's better lads than him about!
I'll wear my buckled slippers out
A-dancing till the break of day.
I'm better off with him away!
And if he never come," said she,
"Now what on earth is that to me?
I wouldn't have him back!"
                    I hope
Her mother washed her mouth with soap.

FRUSTRATION

If I had a shiny gun
I could have a world of fun
Speeding bullets through the brains
Of the folk who give me pains

Or had I some poison gas
I could make the moments pass
Bumping off a number of
People whom I do not love.

But I have no lethal weapon—
Thus does Fate our pleasure step on!
So they still are quick and well
Who should be, by rights, in hell.

HEALED

Oh, when I flung my heart away,
    The year was at its fall.
I saw my dear, the other day,
    Beside a flowering wall;
And this was all I had to say:
    "I thought that he was tall!"

LANDSCAPE

Now this must be the sweetest place
    From here to Heaven's end;
The field is white with flowering lace,
    The birches leap and bend,

The hills, beneath the roving sun,
    From green to purple pass,
And little, trifling breezes run
    Their fingers through the grass.

So good it is, so gay it is,
    So calm it is, and pure,
A one whose eyes may look on this
    Must be the happier, sure.

But me—I see it flat and gray
    And blurred with misery,
Because a lad a mile away
    Has little need of me.

POST-GRADUATE

Hope it was that tutored me,
  And Love that taught me more;
And now I learn at Sorrow's knee
  The self-same lore.

VERSES IN THE NIGHT
(After an Evening Spent in Reading the Big Boys)

Honeymoon

> "ponder, darling, these busted statues
> of yon moth-eaten forum be aware."
>
> —E. E. Cummings.

Ponder, darling, these busted statues,
    Be aware of the forum, sweet;
Feel the centuries tearing at youse—
    Don't keep asking me when we eat!

Look, my love, where the hills hang drowsy;
    Cæsar watched them, a-wondering, here.
Get yon goddesses, chipped and lousy—
    Don't be trying to bite my ear!

Child, consider the clouds above you,
    Soft and silly, like baby goats—
Don't keep asking me don't I love you!
    Judas! When will you know your oats?

Triolet

"Her teeth were only accidental stars with a talent for
    squad drill."

—T. S. Eliot.

Her teeth were accidental stars
    With a talent for squad drill;
The Pleiades, Orion, Mars—
Her teeth were accidental stars,
Assured celestial corporal's bars,
    So straight they stood, and still.
Her teeth were accidental stars
    With a talent for squad drill.

Mélange for the Unknown George

"George is a lion. . . .
There is no pope."

—Gertrude Stein.

George is a lion;
    There is no pope;
Death is the scion
    Of the house of Hope.
George is a gazelle;
    There is no Freud;
Charles Parnell
    Looked like Ernest Boyd.
George is a llama;
    There is no stork;
Papa loves Mama
    Like Jews love pork.
There's no Frances Newman—
    In a pig's right eye!
Death is as human
    As a mandrake's cry.
George is a racoon; he
    Insists there is art.
Little Annie Rooney
    Is my sweetheart.

LIEBESTOD

When I was bold, when I was bold—
    And that's a hundred years!—
Oh, never I thought my breast could hold
    The terrible weight of tears.

I said: "Now some be dolorous;
    I hear them wail and sigh,
And if it be Love that play them thus,
    Then never a love will I."

I said: "I see them rack and rue,
    I see them wring and ache,
And little I'll crack my heart in two
    With little the heart can break."

When I was gay, when I was gay—
    It's ninety years and nine!—
Oh, never I thought that Death could lay
    His terrible hand in mine.

I said: "He plies his trade among
    The musty and infirm,
A body so hard and bright and young
    Could never be meat for worm."

"I see him dull their eyes," I said,
    "And still their rattling breath.
And how under God could I be dead
    That never was meant for Death?"

But Love came by, to quench my sleep,
    And here's my sundered heart;
And bitter's my woe, and black, and deep,
    And little I guessed a part.

Yet this there is to cool my breast,
    And this to ease my spell;
Now if I were Love's, like all the rest,
    Then can I be Death's, as well.

And he shall have me, sworn and bound,
    And I'll be done with Love.
And better I'll be below the ground
    Than ever I'll be above.

FOR A FAVORITE GRAND-DAUGHTER

Never love a simple lad,
　　Guard against a wise,
Shun a timid youth and sad,
　　Hide from haunted eyes.

Never hold your heart in pain
　　For an evil-doer;
Never flip it down the lane
　　To a gifted wooer.

Never love a loving son,
　　Nor a sheep astray;
Gather up your skirts and run
　　From a tender way.

Never give away a tear,
　　Never toss and pine;
Should you heed my words, my dear,
　　You're no blood of mine!

DILEMMA

If I were mild and I were sweet,
And laid my heart before your feet,
And took my dearest thoughts to you,
And hailed your easy lies as true;
Were I to murmur "Yes," and then
"How true, my dear," and "Yes," again,
And wear my eyes discreetly down,
And tremble whitely at your frown,
And keep my words unquestioning—
My love, you'd run like anything!

Should I be frail, and I be mad,
And share my heart with every lad,
But beat my head against the floor
What times you wandered past my door;
Were I to doubt, and I to sneer,
And shriek "Farewell!" and still be here,
And break your joy, and quench your trust—
I should not see you for the dust!

THEORY

Into love and out again,
    Thus I went, and thus I go.
Spare your voice, and hold your pen—
    Well and bitterly I know
All the songs were ever sung,
    All the words were ever said;
Could it be, when I was young,
    Some one dropped me on my head?

A FAIRLY SAD TALE

I think that I shall never know
Why I am thus, and I am so.
Around me, other girls inspire
In men the rush and roar of fire,
The sweet transparency of glass,
The tenderness of April grass,
The durability of granite;
But me—I don't know how to plan it.
The lads I've met in Cupid's deadlock
Were—shall we say?—born out of wedlock.
They broke my heart, they stilled my song,
And said they had to run along,
Explaining, so to sop my tears,
First came their parents or careers.
But ever does experience
Deny me wisdom, calm, and sense!
Though she's a fool who seeks to capture
The twenty-first fine, careless rapture,
I must go on, till ends my rope,
Who from my birth was cursed with hope.

A heart in half is chaste, archaic;
But mine resembles a mosaic—
The thing's become ridiculous!
Why am I so? Why am I thus?

THE LAST QUESTION

New love, new love, where are you to lead me?
  All along a narrow way that marks a crooked line.
How are you to slake me, and how are you to feed me?
  With bitter yellow berries, and a sharp new wine.

New love, new love, shall I be forsaken?
  One shall go a-wandering, and one of us must sigh.
Sweet it is to slumber, but how shall we awaken—
  Whose will be the broken heart, when dawn
  comes by?

SUPERFLUOUS ADVICE

Should they whisper false of you,
　　Never trouble to deny;
Should the words they say be true,
　　Weep and storm and swear they lie.

DIRECTIONS FOR FINDING THE BARD

Would you see what I'm like,
    This is what to do:
Drowse and take your time, like
    Camels in a zoo.
Sit you where you are, son;
    Rest you where you lie;
I am never far, son,—
    I'll be coming by.
Watch for Trouble, walking
    All along his course,
Stepping high and stalking
    Like a funeral horse.
See his little friend, there,
    Knee beside his knee;
There's your search's end, there,—
    That'll be me!

Would you want to see me,
    This is what to try:

Stretch you, sweet and dreamy,
    Looking at the sky.
Watch for Gloom, a-wheeling
    Black across the sun,
Gibbering and squealing—
    All the crows in one.
See a little speck, there,
    Side against his side,
Sticking at his neck, there;
    Going for the ride;
Dropping, does he drop, son;
    Looping with him, maybe.
Let your seeking stop, son,—
    That'll be Baby!

BUT NOT FORGOTTEN

I think, no matter where you stray,
That I shall go with you a way.
Though you may wander sweeter lands,
You will not soon forget my hands,
Nor yet the way I held my head,
Nor all the tremulous things I said.
You still will see me, small and white
And smiling, in the secret night,
And feel my arms about you when
The day comes fluttering back again.
I think, no matter where you be,
You'll hold me in your memory
And keep my image, there without me,
By telling later loves about me.

TWO-VOLUME NOVEL

The sun's gone dim, and
  The moon's turned black;
For I loved him, and
  He didn't love back.

POUR PRENDRE CONGÉ

I'm sick of embarking in dories
    Upon an emotional sea.
I'm wearied of playing Dolores
    (A rôle never written for me).

I'll never again like a cub lick
    My wounds while I squeal at the hurt.
No more I'll go walking in public,
    My heart hanging out of my shirt.

I'm tired of entwining me garlands
    Of weather-worn hemlock and bay.
I'm over my longing for far lands—
    I wouldn't give *that* for Cathay.

I'm through with performing the ballet
    Of love unrequited and told.
Euterpe, I tender you *vale;*
    Good-bye, and take care of that cold.

I'm done with this burning and giving
    And reeling the rhymes of my woes.
And how I'll be making my living,
    The Lord in His mystery knows.

FOR A LADY WHO MUST WRITE VERSE

Unto seventy years and seven,
    Hide your double birthright well—
You, that are the brat of Heaven
    And the pampered heir to Hell.

Let your rhymes be tinsel treasures,
    Strung and seen and thrown aside.
Drill your apt and docile measures
    Sternly as you drill your pride.

Show your quick, alarming skill in
    Tidy mockeries of art;
Never, never dip your quill in
    Ink that rushes from your heart.

When your pain must come to paper,
    See it dust, before the day;
Let your night-light curl and caper,
    Let it lick the words away.

Never print, poor child, a lay on
    Love and tears and anguishing,
Lest a cooled, benignant Phaon
    Murmur, "Silly little thing!"

RHYME AGAINST LIVING

If wild my breast and sore my pride,
I bask in dreams of suicide;
If cool my heart and high my head,
I think, "How lucky are the dead!"

WISDOM

This I say, and this I know:
    Love has seen the last of me.
Love's a trodden lane to woe,
    Love's a path to misery.

This I know, and knew before,
    This I tell you, of my years:
Hide your heart, and lock your door.
    Hell's afloat in lovers' tears.

Give your heart, and toss and moan,
    What a pretty fool you look!
I am sage, who sit alone;
    Here's my wool, and here's my book.

Look! A lad's a-waiting there,
    Tall he is and bold, and gay.
What the devil do I care
    What I know, and what I say?

CODA

There's little in taking or giving,
    There's little in water or wine;
This living, this living, this living
    Was never a project of mine.
Oh, hard is the struggle, and sparse is
    The gain of the one at the top,
For art is a form of catharsis,
    And love is a permanent flop,
And work is the province of cattle,
    And rest's for a clam in a shell,
So I'm thinking of throwing the battle—
    Would you kindly direct me to hell?

ALSO BY

DOROTHY PARKER

ENOUGH ROPE
A Book of Light Verse

Known as the wittiest woman in America and a founder
of the fabled Algonquin Round Table, Dorothy Parker
was also one of the Jazz Age's most beloved poets. Her
verbal dexterity and cynical humor were on full display in
the many poems she published in *Vanity Fair*, *The New
Yorker*, and *Life* and collected in her first book in 1926.
The poems in *Enough Rope* range from lighthearted self-
deprecation to acid-tongued satire, all the while gleefully
puncturing sentimental clichés about the relations between
men and women.

Poetry

VINTAGE CLASSICS
Available wherever books are sold.
vintagebooks.com

FLAPPERS AND PHILOSOPHERS
by F. Scott Fitzgerald

Flappers and Philosophers was published in 1920 on the heels of Fitzgerald's sensational debut, *This Side of Paradise*, and anticipated themes in *The Great Gatsby*. This iconic collection marks the writer's entry into short fiction and contains some of his most famous early stories, including "Bernice Bobs Her Hair," "The Ice Palace," "Head and Shoulders," and "The Offshore Pirate." In these pages we meet Fitzgerald's trademark characters: the beautiful, headstrong young women and the dissolute, wandering young men who comprised what came to be called the Lost Generation. With their bobbed hair and dangling cigarettes, his characters are sophisticated, witty, and, above all, modern: the spoiled heiress who falls for her kidnapper, the intellectual student whose life is turned upside down by a chorus girl, the feuding debutantes whose weapons are cutting words and a pair of scissors. An instant classic in its time, this collection evokes 1920s America through the eyes of a writer indelibly linked to that singular era.

Fiction

PARADE'S END
by Ford Madox Ford

Parade's End explores the world of the English ruling class as it descends into the chaos of war. Christopher Tietjens is an officer from a wealthy family who finds himself torn between his unfaithful socialite wife, Sylvia, and his suffragette mistress, Valentine. A profound portrait of one man's internal struggles during a time of brutal world conflict, *Parade's End* bears out Graham Greene's prediction that "There is no novelist of this century more likely to live than Ford Madox Ford."

Fiction

TO THE LIGHTHOUSE
by Virginia Woolf

The enduring power of this iconic classic flows from the brilliance of its narrative technique and the impressionistic beauty of its prose. Though the novel turns on the death of its central figure, Mrs. Ramsay, her presence pervades every page in a poetic evocation of loss and memory that is also a celebration of domestic life and its most intimate details. Observed across the years at their vacation house on the Isle of Skye, Mrs. Ramsay and her family seek to recapture meaning from the flux of things and the passage of time. *To the Lighthouse* enacts a moving allegory of the creative consciousness and its momentary triumphs over fleeting material life.

Fiction

A MENCKEN CHRESTOMATHY
His Own Selection of His Choicest Writings
by H. L. Mencken

Edited and annotated by H. L. M., this is a selection from his out-of-print writings. They come mostly from books—the six installments of the Prejudices series, *A Book of Burlesques, In Defense of Women, Notes on Democracy, Making a President, Damn! A Book of Calumny, Treatise on Right and Wrong*—but there are also magazine and newspaper pieces that never got between covers (from the *American Mercury*, the *Smart Set*, and the *Baltimore Evening Sun*) and some notes that were never previously published at all. Readers will find edification and amusement in his estimates of a variety of Americans—Woodrow Wilson, Aimee Semple McPherson, Roosevelt I and Roosevelt II, James Gibbons Huneker, Rudolph Valentino, Calvin Coolidge, Ring Lardner, Theodore Dreiser, and Walt Whitman. Those musically inclined will enjoy his pieces on Beethoven, Schubert, and Wagner, and there is material for a hundred controversies in his selections on Joseph Conrad, Thorstein Veblen, Nietzsche, and Madame Blavatsky.

Essays

THE SUN ALSO RISES
by Ernest Hemingway

Ernest Hemingway, winner of the Nobel Prize in Literature in 1954, exerted a lasting influence on fiction in English through his economical prose style that conceals more than it reveals. His first novel, published in 1926, is narrated by world-weary journalist Jake Barnes, who is burdened by a wound acquired in World War I and by his utterly hopeless love for the flamboyantly decadent Lady Brett Ashley. *The Sun Also Rises* tracks the Lost Generation of the 1920s from the nightclubs of Paris to the bullfighting arenas of Spain.

Fiction

QUEEN LUCIA & MISS MAPP
by E. F. Benson

E. F. Benson's beloved Mapp and Lucia novels are sparkling, classic comedies of manners set against the petty snobberies and competitive maneuverings of English village society in the 1920s and 1930s. Benson's series revolves around two unforgettable characters, both forceful and irrepressible women who dominate their respective villages in southern England and who will eventually end up hilariously at war with each other. Lucia is the more deadly of the two, with her pretentious tastes, treacherous charm, and lust for power. Miss Elizabeth Mapp, on the other hand, is younger and more forceful and able to terrify her opponents into submission. Benson introduces these splendid comic creations in the first two novels of the series, *Queen Lucia* (1920) and *Miss Mapp* (1922).

Fiction